NEW LIFE

❧

_____
Child's Name

_____
Birth Date

_____
Place of Birth

❧

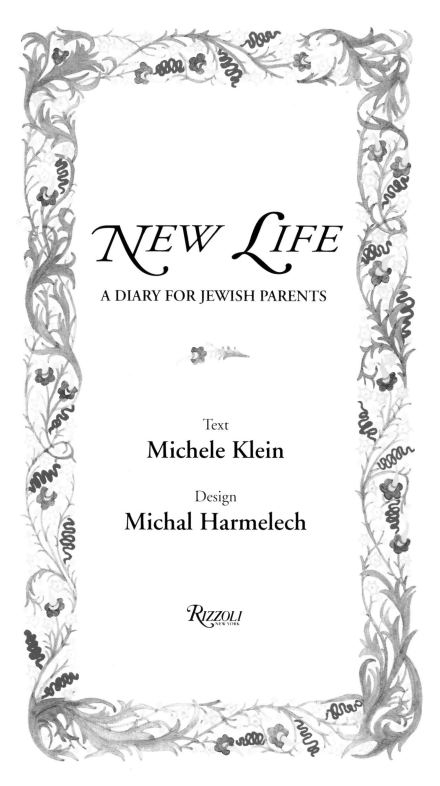

NEW LIFE

A DIARY FOR JEWISH PARENTS

Text
Michele Klein

Design
Michal Harmelech

RIZZOLI
NEW YORK

Front cover illustration:
A lullaby, "Rozhinkes mit Mandeln",
Zeev Raban, Jerusalem, circa 1935

First published in the United Sates of America in 1992
by Rizzoli International Publications, Inc.
300 Park Avenue South
New York, New York 10010

ISBN 0-8478-5633-X
92 93 94 95 96/10 9 8 7 6 5 4 3 2 1

Printed and bound in Hong Kong

"THE CHILD WILL GIVE YOU NEW LIFE..."
(Ruth 4:15)

*I*n the beginning . . . God blessed Adam and Eve on the day of their creation with the promise of children. In Jewish tradition, children are a blessing; their nurturing and education has always been of utmost importance. A baby provides hope for the future, for the continuation of the family and, in a wider context, for the Jewish people too. Throughout the long history of the Jewish people, a baby's birth has been celebrated by rituals that welcome the baby into the Jewish community. Some of these are dictated by the Bible, others became popular in Talmudic times, in the Middle Ages, or in more recent times. While often they have religious significance, they all serve to strengthen the family's sense of Jewish identity. Some of the customs that were practised in the past were in fact strategies to cope with the fears surrounding childbearing and rearing. They were given Jewish character by association with God and the Bible or by interpretation in terms of Jewish philosophy. Yet still today a pregnant woman seeks information to reduce her anxieties about her baby. In labor she appreciates a few words of comfort in her ear; a newborn is greeted with "mazal tov"; and parents are actively involved in educating their children.

We have chosen a few illustrations, from a large selection, to impart a feeling of continuity in the profound experiences of childbearing and childrearing, from the distant past to the present day. While the rich folklore surrounding childbirth is disappearing in the face of modern medicine, parenting still involves happiness and disappointments, pride and pain, hopes and anxieties, responsibility and commitment.

We hope this book will stimulate parents to note and preserve some of their own experiences with their child. It is up to the parent to decide if she or he will note simply the milestones in their child's early life, or whether the blank spaces are filled with the ups and downs of childraising. This book may serve to record happy moments of childhood, or witticisms and clever remarks that come when least expected; it may reveal the emotions that flow inevitably, decisions about sleep problems, tantrums, or separation anxieties. Other ideas are provided. Here, there is room to store memories that might not fit into a photograph album.

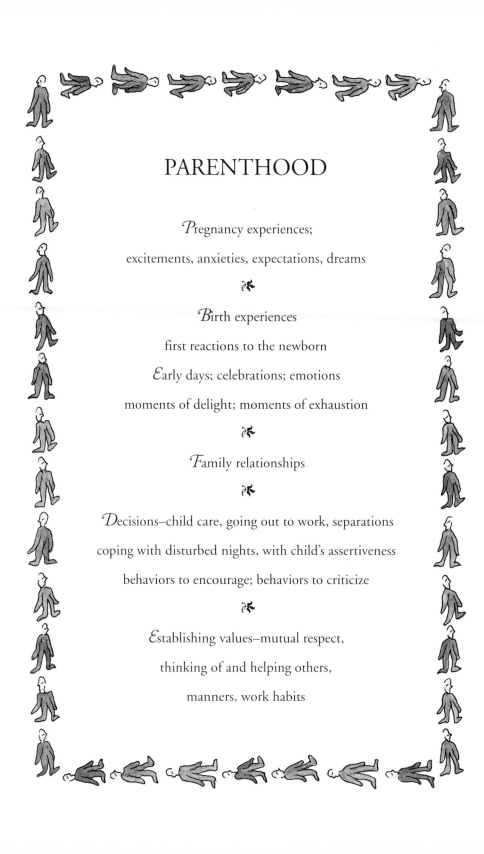

PARENTHOOD

*P*regnancy experiences;

excitements, anxieties, expectations, dreams

❧

*B*irth experiences

first reactions to the newborn

*E*arly days; celebrations; emotions

moments of delight; moments of exhaustion

❧

*F*amily relationships

❧

*D*ecisions–child care, going out to work, separations

coping with disturbed nights, with child's assertiveness

behaviors to encourage; behaviors to criticize

❧

*E*stablishing values–mutual respect,

thinking of and helping others,

manners, work habits

CHILDHOOD

*W*atches, smiles, turns over, sits,

crawls, stands, first steps

❧

*F*irst tooth appears; first tooth falls

first words; funny phrases

*I*dentifies colors; draws a face; counts

❧

*S*leeping; dreams

❧

*L*ikes and dislikes–food, clothes, friends, games, stories

*E*xpressions of independence

*E*motions–love, frustration, jealousy, fears

*C*ute remarks; difficult questions

❧

*T*ransitions–starting school, birth of a sibling

*C*oping with authority–parents, teachers

*S*ocial life

וְרַב כְּמָה שְׁנֵי רִבְבָה
כִּצְמַח חַהַשָׂרֶה
נְתַתִּיךְ וַתִּרְבִּי וַתִּגְדְּלִי
וַתָּבֹאִי בַּעֲדִי עֲדָיִים
שָׂדַיִים נָכֹנוּ וּשְׂעָרֵךְ

Woman giving birth to six children.
Dragon Haggada, France, thirteenth century.

𝒯he world was created for habitation and traditional
Judaism considers it the duty and joy of every man to "be
fruitful and multiply" (Gen. 1:28). Children are a blessing,
promising continuity for the Jewish family and the
whole Jewish people.

A pregnant woman consults two sages about the baby's future.
Yahuda Haggada, Germany, fifteenth century.

There is an element of anxious uncertainty in every pregnancy, today as in the past. One way of overcoming this is to seek predictions. In the past, forecasts were sometimes made by divination, for example from a Bible opened at random.

Dream interpretation.
Liturgical collection, Italy, fifteenth century.

Since ancient times Jews have interpreted dreams, either as
indicating events of the day or as visions of future
events. While today dreams sometimes are understood to
bear messages from the unconscious, in the past dreams
were thought to bear supernatural communications, from
God or, on occasion, from demons.

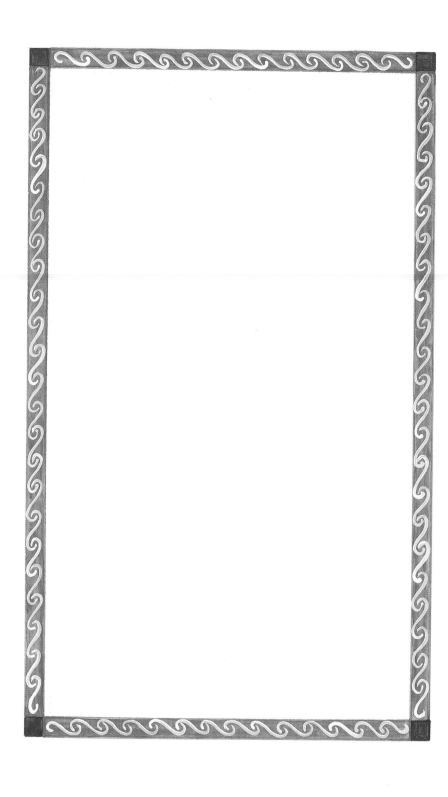

Rebekah gives birth to Esau and Jacob.
Sarajevo Haggada, Spain, fourteenth century.

Jewish birth helpers offered both physical and emotional
support. The names of the Biblical midwives suggest their
differing roles: Puah might have calmed the cries of the
laboring woman, encouraging her with kind words,
a prayer or incantation, while Shifrah concerned herself
with the baby's reception.

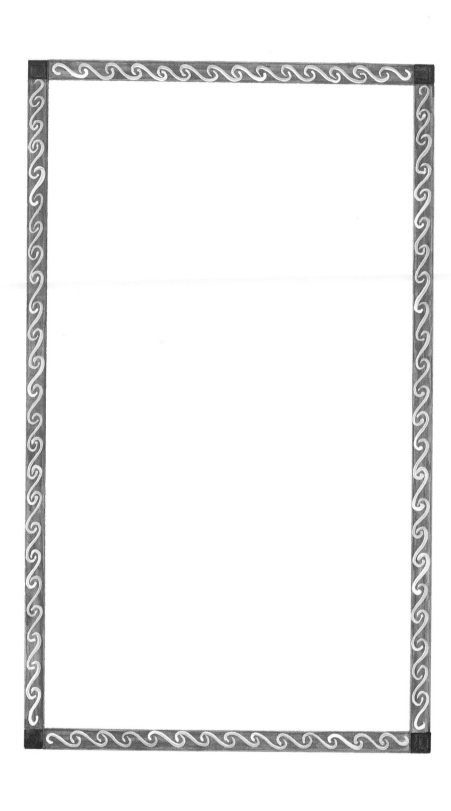

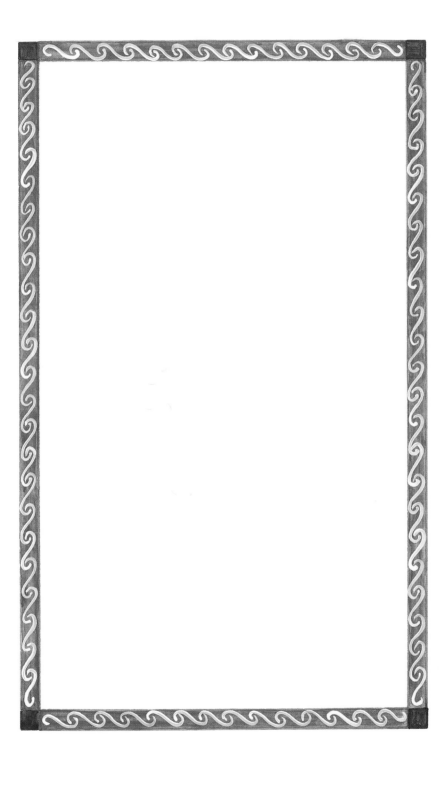

Childbed amulet.
Carpathian Mountains, nineteenth century.

Since antiquity Jews have fashioned amulets with inscrip-
tions against a demon that harms birthing women and
their newborn. An early legend tells of such a demon,
Lilith, who was Adam's first wife. She fled after a quarrel,
but was caught by three angels, Sanui, Sansanui and
Samengulf. To save her life, she promised not to harm any-
one protected by an amulet inscribed with the
names of these angels.

וסנסיני וסמבלף · סיני וסנסיני וסמב

Lying-in.
Harrison Miscellany, Italy, eighteenth century.

If mother and baby were well, the first week after birth
was time for celebration. Visitors brought gifts, money, or
special foods and lights were kept burning, for rejoicing
as well as keeping away evil spirits. During this period,
mother and baby were never left unattended. Since
the Middle Ages, a father of a baby boy might celebrate
the first Friday eve and the night before the
circumcision, as well as the ritual itself.

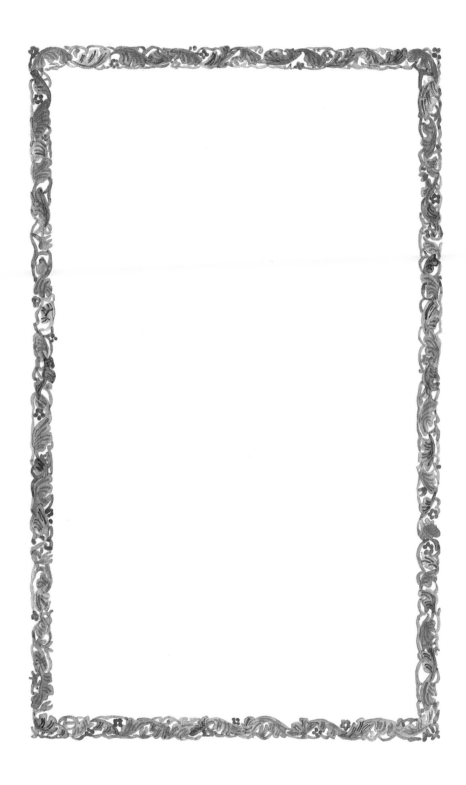

Yocheved, nurse of the Hebrew women.
Breslau Haggada, Germany, 1768.

*I*n the Biblical story, Miriam tells Pharaoh's daughter that
she knows of a Hebrew wet-nurse; thus baby Moses was
brought to nurse at the breast of his mother, Yocheved.

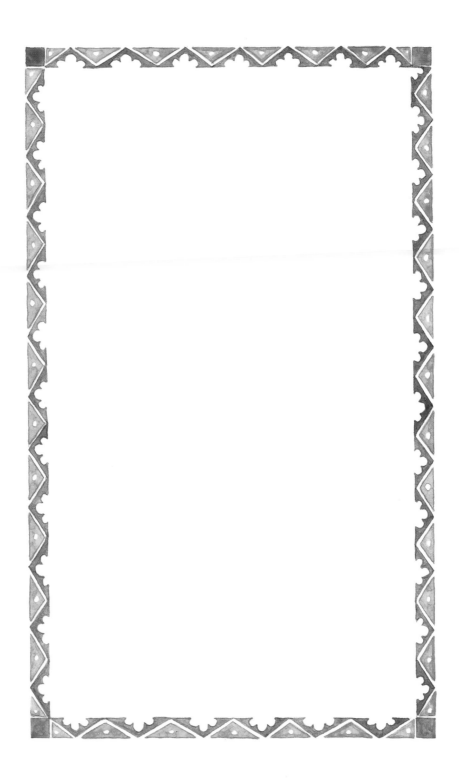

Abraham circumcises Isaac.
Regensburg Bible, Germany, circa 1300.

"Every male among you shall be circumcised . . .
and that shall be the sign of the covenant between Me
and you. And throughout the generations, every
male among you shall be circumcised at the
age of eight days." (Gen. 17:10-12).

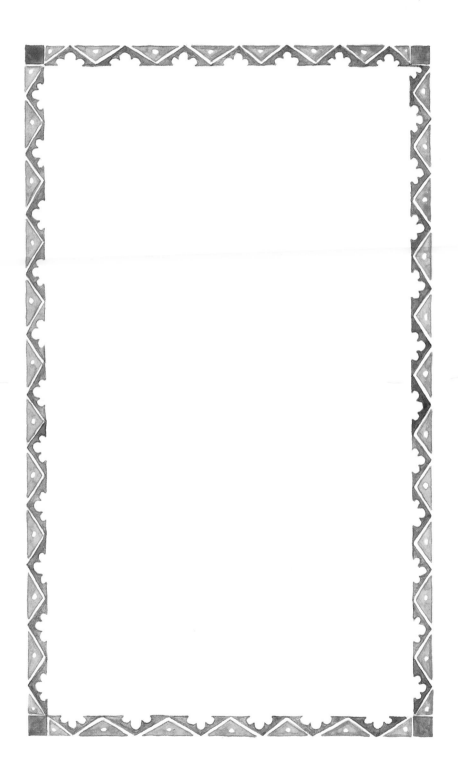

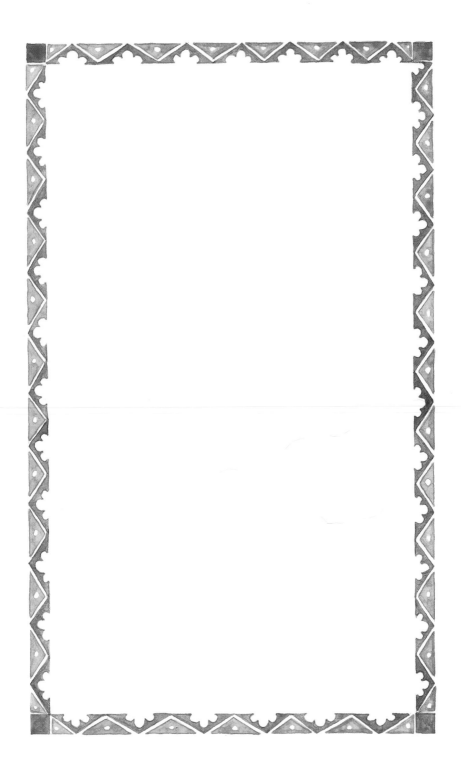

Baby girl naming ceremony, "Hollekreisch".
Liturgical manuscript, South Germany, 1589.

*I*n many Jewish communities girls were named
ceremoniously. The "Hollekreisch" gathering, where the cradle
was raised to the announcement of the baby's name, dates from
medieval times. The Jews of Spain celebrated the birth of a
daughter before the Inquisition, continuing in their new homes
after the Expulsion. And the Jews of the Orient often greeted a
newborn daughter with blessings and festivities.

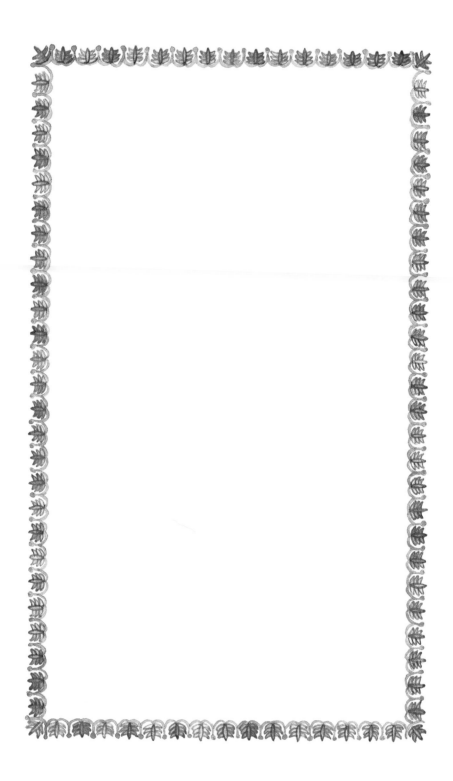

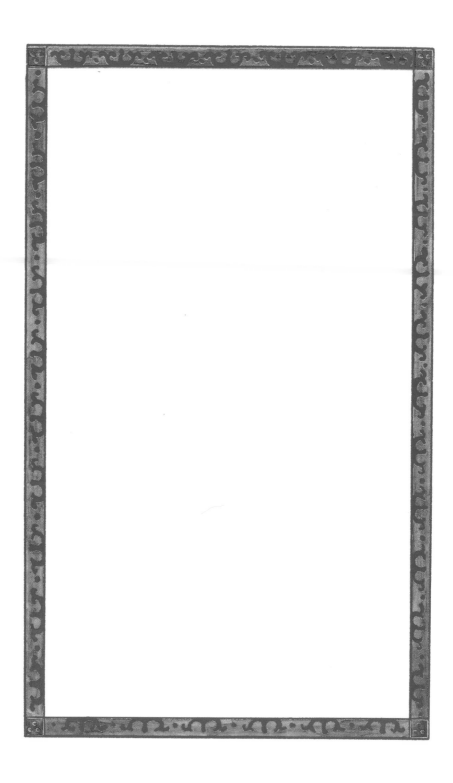

עבד פטר חמר בכל

Redemption of the first-born.
Liturgical manuscript, Italy, fifteenth century.

❦

"You shall have the first-born of man redeemed . . . Take
as their redemption price, from the age of one month up,
the money equivalent of five shekels by the sanctuary
weight . . ." (Numb. 18:15-16).

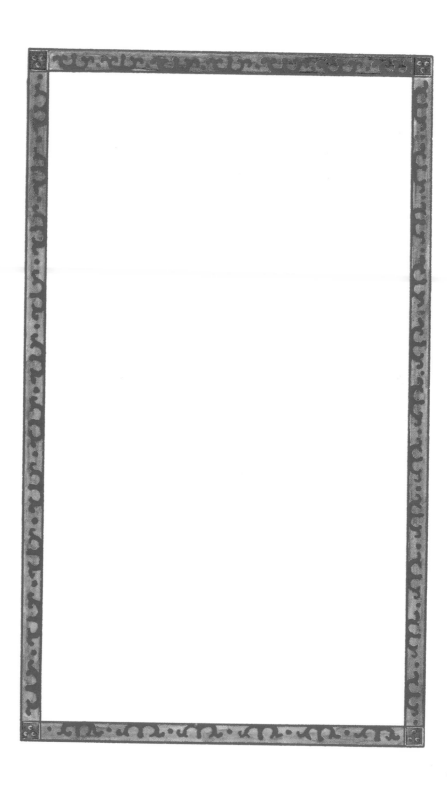

Family record.
Isaac S. Wachman, U.S.A., 1922.

Jews were noting their children's births long before the first
laws about registering births were issued. In the late
Middle Ages, a father might inscribe the births in his
family on the leaf of a book he owned – a custom that
continued until the late nineteenth century. Circumcisers
kept registers of circumcisions they performed, providing
registers of male births in their district.

A lullaby, "Rozhinkes mit Mandeln".
Zeev Raban, Jerusalem, circa 1935.

*B*y depicting the Yiddish lullaby as being sung by a
Yemenite mother, the artist attempted to integrate East and
West Jewish cultures.

קשת ★ גדי ★ דלי ★ דגים ★ טלה ★ שור ★ תאומים ★ סרטן ★ אריה ★ בתולה ★ מאזנים ★ עקרב

Jews study the stars.
Maimonides' Code, Italy, circa 1450.

𝒯he Hebrew word "mazal" – "star" or "constellation" – has
come to mean "luck" through the historical popularity of
astrology, and today the announcement of a baby's birth is
often greeted with "mazal tov", in the hope that the infant
was born with good luck – under a lucky star.

קשת ★ גדי ★ דלי ★ דגים ★ טלה

קשת ★ גדי ★ דלי ★ דגים ★ טלה

המזלות בדרך ★ בולם ★ מעגלם ★ בתורה ירח ★ וסטר

A Jewish babe.
Rothschild Miscellany. Italy, circa 1470.

When does a baby begin to learn? According to Jewish legend, the soul of the baby in the womb learns the entire Torah and lives in light and happiness. When it is time to go out into the world, an angel warns the little soul that it will eventually have to give an account of itself before God.

The soul protests and the angel strikes the baby, extinguishing the light, thereby causing the soul to forget all its prenatal knowledge. Education begins after birth, to regain all that was learnt in the womb.

A child takes his first steps,
guided by his mother and grandfather.
Book of Fables, Germany, 1450.

*C*hildren mature gradually, passing from one milestone to the next, each at his own pace. Until he is one year old, a child is like a king and everyone embraces him. Until two or three years of age, the child is like a pig, crawling on the floor and putting his hands into everything dirty. At ten, he jumps around like a goat and at eighteen he is like a horse, rejoicing in his youth and strength. When he marries he is like a donkey carrying a burden. When he becomes a father he runs around like a dog to provide food for his family, and in old age he is like a monkey, as no one pays attention to his caprices.

אבגדהוזחטיכך למםנןסעפף

Textbook for teaching the alphabet to children.
Oriental, tenth century.

·אב·

The rabbis taught that when a child is three years old and
speaking he should be ready to learn the alphabet. But,
they added, each child should be allowed to develop at his
own pace, and lessons may be postponed until the child is
sufficiently mature. While it is a father's obligation to see
that his child is educated according to Jewish law, both
parents have a role in shaping his emotional, moral, and
intellectual development.

אבגדהוזחטיכך למםנסעפף

אבגדהוזחטיכך למםנסעפף

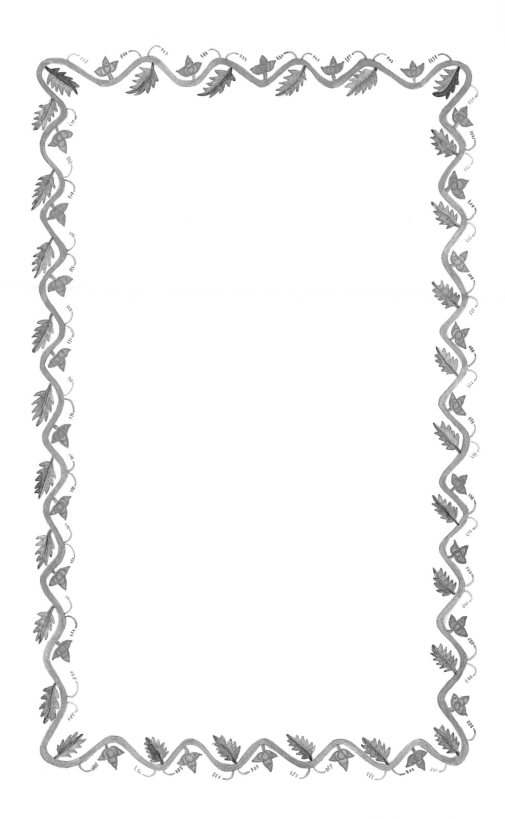

Jewish child at his lesson, master with whip, hourglass
to measure tuition time.
Coburg Bible, Germany, late fourteenth century.

Education is achieved through the occasional reprimand,
as well as love and praise. Disciplining a child is considered
the duty of every parent and teacher, even if it is
distressing; it is only through discipline that a child learns
responsibility and self-control.

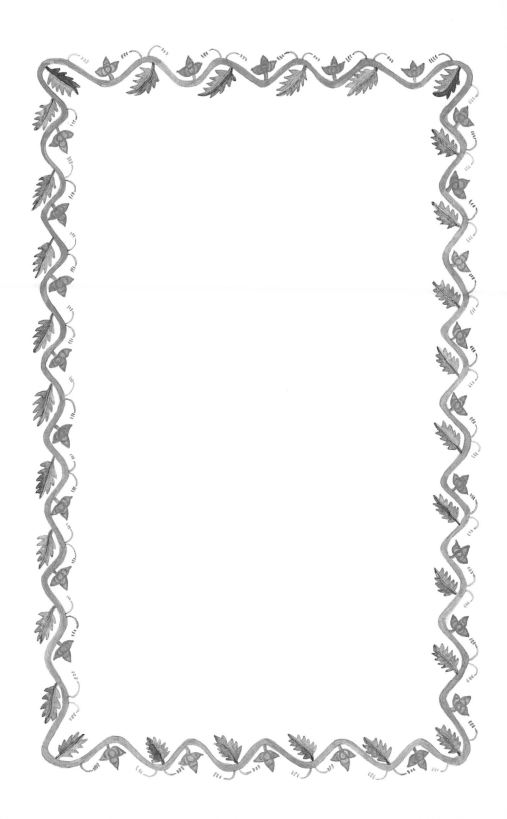

Jacob blesses his grandsons, Ephraim and Menasseh.
Golden Haggada, Spain, fourteenth century.

*I*n old age, Jacob blessed his grandsons before blessing his own
sons; he cherished his grandsons more than his sons. Joseph
lived long enough to enjoy his great-grandchildren sitting in his
lap. Many fathers had little time for playing with their young
children, while later in life they had time to enjoy their
grandchildren, even great-grandchildren.

Brotherly love.
Castillian Haggadah, Spain, fourteenth century.

The Bible provides many examples of sibling rivalry, often due
to parental favoritism toward one child. These examples serve
as a warning to parents to treat their children equally. The
compassion, honor, love, and faithfulness that begin in the
home form the foundation for the child's growing personality.

The marriage canopy.
Liturgical manuscript, South Germany, sixteenth century.

The traditional desires of Jewish parents are that their children
should grow up to the study of Torah, to do good deeds, and to
the marriage canopy. In Talmudic times the marriage canopy
was sometimes made from a few branches of cedar and pine,
from the trees that were planted at the birth of the
groom and bride.

MEMORABILIA

Photographs

Drawings, self-portraits

❧

Footprint, handprint, or name tag

❧

Lock of hair

❧

First signature, a letter

Family trees

❧

List of gifts

Certificates

ACKNOWLEDGMENTS

*W*e would like to thank the following libraries, museums and private collectors for permitting the reproduction of works in their collections. The acknowledgments are listed in the order in which the reproductions appear in this book. All the miniatures are taken from illuminated manuscripts, except the lullaby by Zeev Raban, the childbed amulet, and the family record (painted by Isaac S. Wachman).

Woman giving birth to six children, Cod. Heb. 155, f. 23v., Hamburg State and University Library; pregnant woman consults two sages, Yahuda Haggada, fol. 31v., Israel Museum; dream interpretation, Garrett Ms. 26, f. 28r., Princeton University Library; birth scene, Sarajevo Castillian Haggada, f. 9v., Sarajevo National Museum; childbed amulet, JMS 14, Jewish Museum of Switzerland, Basel, photo D. Widmer; lying-in, Harrison Misc., Sotheby's New York; nurse of Hebrew women, Heb. 8º2340, f. 27r., Jewish National University Library; circumcision, Regensburg Bible, f. 18v., Israel Museum; baby girl naming, Ms. No. Hs. 7058, f. 44r., German National Museum, Nürnberg; redemption of firstborn, Garrett Ms. 26, f. 8., Princeton University Library; Wachman Family Record, collection of Francisco F. Sierra, New York, NY., photo courtesy Museum of American Folk Art, New York, NY; "Rozhinkes mit Mandeln" of Zeev Raban, collection Philip Goodman, Jerusalem, photo Y.Brill, Beth Hatefutsoth; Jews study the stars, Cod. Rossian 498, f. 13v., Bibliotheca Apostolica Vaticana; a Jewish babe, Rothschild Misc. 24, f. 246r. detail, Israel Museum; first steps, Cod. Hebr. 107, f. 79v., Bayerische Staatsbibliothek; alphabet textbook, T-S K5.13 r. and v., of the Cambridge University Library, courtesy of the Syndics of the C.U.L.; child's lesson, Add. 19776, f. 72v., The British Library; blessing grandchildren, Add. 27210, f. 8v., The British Library; brotherly love, Or. 2737, f. 68r., The British Library; wedding, Ms. No. Hs. 7058, f. 34v., German National Museum, Nürnberg.